Nikola Tesla

A Forgotten Genius

Savy Gill

TS Gill

Vik Gill

Copyright 2018

Dedicated

To

Emma Lazarus

For capturing the spirit that is America

"Give me your tired, your poor,
Your huddled masses yearning to breathe
free,
The wretched refuse of your teeming shore.
Send these, the homeless, tempest-tossed, to
me:
I lift my lamp beside the golden door."

Table of Contents

Preface

Around the turn of the last century circa 1900, Nikola Tesla was one of the most well-known scientists in the world. Everyone knew him as the genius that had made it possible to bring electricity to every home and factory.

After his death in 1943 however, his memory soon faded from the public mind and the role of his ideas in everyday life was forgotten.

Recently, however, Tesla's fame and luster has found a new shine. In an inspired act of deference and grace, Elon Musk has named his new electric car company, Tesla. This is a fitting tribute to the man who was known as the wizard of electricity.

People are also enamored by his underdog status and his creed of battling gargantuan forces in a quest to help the ordinary man and woman.

These inspired few are picking up from where Tesla left off. They are once again challenging the rusty paradigms of limitation and are looking boldly into all that is possible for advancing us forward into a better future.

A few examples include people such as Elon Musk, Richard Branson, Jeff Bezos, the late Steve Jobs, Bill Gates and others. They have rekindled the hopeful idealism of Tesla's time and are daring to take risks on unique projects that others would consider foolhardy.

Some success has already been achieved by their efforts. They have taken computers from giant boxes the size of rooms to being equally powerful but still versatile and convenient as cellphones and watches. They have made the launching of space rockets and space exploration by an individual possible. One of them has successfully eradicated a disease that ravaged humanity for millennia in a certain part of the world. These are but just a few of the many accomplishments of the new idealists.

Some people have called Elon Musk a modern-day incarnation of both Tesla and Thomas Edison. He also likes to dream big as they did and has plans to help humanity survive by making solar power cheap, electric cars affordable and space travel possible. More on this later.

In addition to inspiring individuals such as Elon Musk, Tesla also left the world with a wealth of ideas for posterity. These were forgotten at the time of his death, but they are now being looked at again with fresh eyes. Many are finding that he was ahead of his times by decades and that his ideas are still worth exploring. Some of his notes and patents are still classified as top secret.

A better way to understand why Tesla continues to hold mass appeal might be to look at his personal qualities. Tesla was at his heart a kind and generous soul. He held egalitarian views and believed that human beings should work together and help each other. He did not believe in plundering the earth's precious resources, and he was opposed to unbridled greed. He wanted to bring prosperity and freedom to all of humanity and not a greedy heartless few. He had visions of providing free electricity to all human beings.

Regarding his personal life, Tesla remained a private and enigmatic individual. He only socialized sporadically and preferred solitude and nature over crowds. He did endear himself however to those that knew him. They fawned over him and liked his honest manner and the simple predictability of his rigid habits. This seeming remoteness has only added to the myth of his personality and his allure.

This book takes a look at the life of this complicated man and provides brief snapshots of his ideas, actions, and visions. It was written with the hope that understanding him might yield clues to what made him succeed where he did and what his limitations were. Wherever possible, some take away lessons are drawn that some may find useful for improving productivity in their own lives.

As a side note, it is important to remember in times of rhetoric and promoted xenophobia, that Nikola Tesla was an immigrant from Serbia. It was his inventions and ideas that gave America a head start and taught us how to harness hydroelectric energy and transmit it long distances in order to turn the machines in our factories. This is what in turn made the United States an economic and industrial powerhouse that it became in the 20th century.

Albert Einstein was another immigrant who enriched America. He advanced understanding about the universe at a very fundamental level. He showed that matter, energy and time were related. His theory of relativity allowed for the conception of the ultimate weapon in the form of the atom bomb. This bomb in turn was the only thing that stopped the fascist forces of Japan and its allies from taking over much of the world.

There have been other great immigrants that have enriched America as well. America has been made great by opening our arms to such immigrants. These are people that to escape tyranny or are merely looking to build a better life for themselves and their families. They are no different than the first pilgrims that came to America.

Instead of being a liability the immigrant population in America has been a huge asset to our nation. They have made positive strides and contributions to every walk of life. They are truly the brawn in America's might.

Our greatness and glory thus lies not in our isolation but our open embrace of those who seek our shores for a better life.

This does not mean that we should allow habitual criminals with a history of violence or antisocial conduct into the country. We should, however, keep the influx of immigrants open to those who are law-abiding and want to pursue a better life. Such an open-door policy to talent and the immigrant quest may yield us another Tesla or Einstein. A person that could save America and the world yet again!

The Authors

<u>Some</u> of the Patents and Inventions of Nikola Tesla

The below list highlights the extent of Tesla's contributions to science and engineering.

1. Successfully Created the Alternating Current Motor
2. Developed The Ability To Transmit Alternating Current Over Long Distances
3. Discovery Of X-Rays
4. Discovery Of Radio Waves
5. Discovery Of Wireless Transmission
6. Developing A Better Arc Lamp
7. Commutator For Dynamoelectric Machines
8. Regulator For Dynamoelectric Machines
9. Dynamo Electric Machine
10. Electromagnetic Motor
11. System Up Electrical Distribution
12. Electrical Transmission Of Power
13. Electromagnetic Motor
14. Method Of Operating Electromagnetic Motors
15. Method Of Electrical Power Transmission
16. Method Of Direct Current From Alternating Currents
17. Pyromagneto Electric Generator
18. Alternating Current Electromagnetic Motor
19. Electrical Transformer Or Induction Device
20. Method Of Operating Arc – Lamps
21. Alternating Current Generator

Birth and Early Life

The above picture shows the idyllic childhood home of the pensive young Nikola Tesla. He was born in the old Austro-Hungarian Empire that is now modern-day Croatia. His birthplace was a small high plateau village called Smiljan. They say that he was born at the stroke of midnight between July 9 and July 10, 1856. At the hour of his birth, a lightning storm was raging in the night. Bolts of lightning arched in the dark night and deafening peals of thunder rolled over the hills. This was the actual weather on the night of his birth and it is not a mere apocryphal story. It was as if nature itself was announcing the birth of a great man that would later come to be known as the wizard of electricity and lightning. It also served as a beautiful motif for his life's work as he left the world in awe with his brilliant innovations and flashes of insight.

The midwife however worried that his birth at such an hour was a sign of ill omen. Nikola's mother was wise and corrected the midwife saying that it was a good omen instead and that her son would be "a child of the light."

Nikola's early childhood was spent running and playing with his friends in the woods and streams nearby. He was a happy child and curious about all things.

He was like the other kids of the village but he wasn't your typical boy growing up. For one, he did not like to be closely held or kissed by relatives and had a detached and objective manner of rendering his opinions. For example, when asked in jest which one of his aunts was prettier, he pointed to one and said that she was less ugly.

In addition to his unusual, perhaps overly honest tendencies, he had a natural affinity with nature and was fascinated with creatures both large and small. His father, a strict but kind Orthodox priest at the local parish, was distant but affectionate towards Tesla. He was deeply religious and wanted Nikola to become a priest like him.

When Nikola was about five years old, a deep tragedy struck his family. His older brother Daniel was thrown from a beautiful Arabian riding horse that the family owned. The boy was badly wounded and later succumbed to his wounds. This event was to cast a long shadow over the entire family but more acutely over Nikola's childhood. Daniel had also been a gifted child of great potential, and the parents grieved his loss for a long time.

The effect of this dynamic on Nikola has been the object of speculation for some psychoanalysts. They have opined that this conflict may have been the cause of obsessive-compulsive traits in Tesla. He developed these they say to soothe and undo the guilt about triggering the parent's sorrow by reminding them of Daniel by his own success. It is just one of the theories. We now know that there can be many other causes of obsessive behaviors including an immune response to the common sore throat infection.

There is no doubt that Nikola's mother, Djuka doted on him and was a good and kind woman. She was also brilliant in her own right and is said to have had a photographic memory. It is said that she was able to create tools and inventions for the home and her garden. She created these to save work and make her life easier. Nikola Tesla adopted this mindset for his own inventions later on.

His father's name was Milutin, and he served as a model of decorum and erudition. He was idealistic, well read and spoke several languages. He received an award for his inspirational sermons. He often tried to link scriptures with philosophy and other systems of thought. He could hold his own in a debate, and people respected his opinions on all things, both big and small.

The Tesla family was a big clan, and they were well respected in the community. There were several distinguished and influential men and women that were born in the family on both the mother and the father's side of the family. One of Nikola's nephews would later immigrate to the United States and also create multiple patents and inventions. Another descendant in the family would later become the Yugoslav ambassador to the United States.

As he was growing up, young Nikola was an avid reader. He read almost all the books in his father's well stocked library at a young age. His appetite for reading was so voracious that Nikola's father worried about the effect on his eyesight. He, therefore, forbade him from reading at night by candlelight and also removed the candles from his room. Tesla found a way around this and began to make candles in his room. He also began to cover the door sills at the bottom with old clothes to prevent any light from leaving his room when his father expected his room to be dark and for him to be asleep.

He was a natural scientist and tried his hand at backyard experiments. He was also a visual thinker and methodical in his approach to solving problems. At times, flashes of insight would come upon him and provide him with unique ways of resolving the pesky questions and problems that he had been working on. The result was that Nikola Tesla excelled in problem-solving and enjoyed the thrill of finding a solution.

He was a keen observer of nature and often extrapolated ideas from everyday observations and applied them to the larger phenomenon of nature. As a child, when he noticed sparks and crackles after stroking the fur of his cat, he surmised, correctly that the clouds were like the arched back of a giant cat that the movement of fast air stroked like a giant hand, and that the was lightning and thunder were similar to the crackles and sparks that he observed when he stroked his cat.

He was observant and came up with unique devices and inventions. One such example was some special hooks he designed to lure frogs and catch them when ordinary hooks he used for fishing would not work. He also made use of the flapping wings of June bugs to create an engine powered by their wing beats.

He had the pluck and daring to act on his ideas. The following incident serves as an example of the fearlessness that Nikola displayed at crucial moments. In the small town where his family lived, the Mayor and the Fire Chief were inaugurating a new firefighting system to the people of the town. The new fire truck was supposed to pump water from the local river to put out fires when needed, and both were feeling quite proud of having set up this system. There was a problem, however, as no water came from the firehose when the Mayor threw the switch. Nikola had a flash of insight thinking the pipe may be kinked. He dove into the freezing river and proceeded to undo the kink that he actually did find in the hose. With this correction, the water shot out of the firehose, the people were relieved and an embarrassing moment for the Mayor and the Fire Chief had been averted. Nikola quickly earned the respect of these gentlemen and more importantly of his father. The father gave him more leeway from then on when Nikola was distracted during the church services.

An interesting and mysterious phenomenon of a different nature seems to have also been a part of Nikola's early life. This was the experiencing of what can only be described as visual hallucinations that would begin as flashes of light and then be followed by a procession of scenes and images that seemed to almost be like a movie being played for him. He was made anxious by this at first, but his sisters assured him it was ok for him to experience this and they would sit by him as he went through the experience. They even encouraged him to enjoy the scenery and images that appeared before him. He took this advice to heart and began to take on a fantasy life of imagining he was traveling to different countries and meeting the various people that he saw. He did not talk about this to others but admitted in later life that he was continuing to experience such imagery as he did in his childhood.

It is not difficult to understand why Nikola had a refined visual memory of objects in his surroundings and in his memory. He could, for example, hold a three-dimensional image of an object in his mind and turn it any which way he wanted. He used this ability when he designed his innovations in what he called the mental laboratory of his mind. His visualizations were filled with great detail and he could remember them perfectly due to his photographic memory.

Such innovations were designed visually in a precise and exacting manner. He would then turn these into drawings and then have them manufactured as he had visualized them. People were surprised when they would work flawlessly the very first time he gave them a trial run.

Nikola performed brilliantly at school as was expected by his family members and others that knew him. His learning was not merely the rote memory of a savant. He was a deep thinker and had flashes of insight that were greater than the sum of the knowledge that he had gathered.

The Country of His Birth

= Smiljan- Birth Place of Nikola Tesla in modern day Croatia

Tesla hailed from a region known nowadays as Croatia and Serbia. This area of the world has been roiled by battles and conflicts over the centuries between different groups of people. In the tumult and chaos of history, only the strong and smart have survived. To this day, it remains a melting pot of different people and cultures that have learned to coexist in a tenuous peace.

At the time of Tesla's emigration to the United States, Croatia was still part of the Austro-Hungarian Empire. After World War I, the different confederacies of this region came together under the flag of Yugoslavia.

Marshal Josep Tito became the new head of the state and ruled the country with great skill. He used a mix of muscle and diplomacy. He was able to gain international respect for Yugoslavia as he became one of the founders of the Non-Aligned Movement. This was a league of nations that chose to neither ally with the Soviet Union and Communism or the Western Powers and the creed of unbridled Capitalism.

Marshal Josep Tito died in 1980 and Yugoslavia gradually disintegrated into warring factions yet again. There was blood in the streets as the different groups fought for supremacy. Finally, per the Succession Agreement of 2001, the former Yugoslavia was divided into the following 5 states.

1. Serbia and Montenegro
2. Croatia
3. Slovenia
4. Macedonia
5. Bosnia and Herzegovina.

A truce has existed since then, and the 5 republics seem to coexist at this time without too much conflict with each other. This is a peace that has been long awaited.

Tesla's Near-Death Experience

Tesla graduated from High School in 1873 with exemplary scholarships, distinguished himself to his teachers and earned excellent grades. The future course of his career was not clear, and Tesla did not want to become a priest despite his father's insistence that he join the seminary for this purpose. Tesla dreamed of using his facility with mathematics and science to pursue a career as a scientist.

With this decision still hanging over his head, he returned in the same year to his hometown. His parents had told him to stay away because of an epidemic of cholera, but he missed his family and decided to go home anyway.

Unfortunately, he soon contracted Cholera just as his parents had feared. The cycle of transmission of this deadly disease through the contaminated water was not known or understood, and many people died of cholera in those days.

Tesla became quite ill and very dehydrated and weak. He could hardly get up from his bed at this time. He could have died from his protracted illness and his father grew worried. In a rare father-son moment, Tesla asked his father to let him pursue higher studies in the Sciences and not to push the career of clergy upon him. His father thought a promise of this nature might aid his recovery told him he would support his decision and would also send him to the best colleges in the region to study engineering and science, just as Nikola desired. Tesla is reported to have had a miraculous recovery from his illness after receiving this assurance and pledge of support from his father.

After his recovery from cholera, another threat began to loom on the horizon. There was mandatory conscription the next year in 1874 for possible war, and Tesla was a prime candidate for conscription. At the bidding of his family who feared for his life in warfare, he was asked to lay low and hide in the forests for some time. So, Tesla took off for the forests for about a year. He survived by hunting and gathering what he could and reminisced about his closeness with nature during this period.

Early Excellence

Tesla read whatever he could lay his hands on, and his mind was like a sponge that absorbed it all. He enjoyed being in nature and was fascinated with the forces of nature. He experienced vivid visual hallucinations and came to accept these as adventures or waking dreams.

He had a diverse range of interests and read a range of books. These included books on poetry, adventure tales, and short stories. He loved the works of Mark Twain as they resonated with some of his own adventures in the Serbian countryside. He would later become good friends with Mark Twain when he later moved to America.

A book he read in his childhood made a forceful impact on him. It was a small novel called Abafi by the Hungarian author Miklos Josika and translated into Serbian. In this book, the protagonist is a nobleman called Oliver Abafi who overcomes his earlier hedonism and wayward ways with a firm resolution and will. The hero than goes on to elevate himself to a nobleman worthy of respect and honor. The book made him believe that a resolute will and determined purpose can help one overcome any hurdle in life.

Nikola demonstrated this force of will time and again. He could work for long hours on projects that he has had an interest in. He worked very long hours and would become totally immersed in his work for up to 17 to 20 hours at a time. He seemed to need very little sleep and was up and ready to work after a short sleep of 2 to 3 hours. He was powered by his purpose and did not feel he was at work when he was in the grip of a fascinating project. He believed in the view that the work of giving form to his ideas was the highest calling of his life and a service to God.

When Nikola Tesla enrolled in the Austrian Polytechnic in Graz Austria, he excelled in all his studies. He kept long hours and spent many days in the local library reading up on all that was available on the subjects related to electrical engineering. He would often read works in different languages to get different perspectives. The result of all this hard work were grades that soared far above of any of the other students at his college. His professors were hugely impressed and praised his intellect but were worried about his physical health. They even wrote to his father about what a brilliant man his son Nikola was but that the father should see to it that he takes better care of his health.

Tesla studied here for about 3 years but did not officially graduate for reasons that are yet totally clear.

He is said to have from a period of nervous exhaustion. He broke off contact with his family for a period of time and worked as a draftsman for a very meager pay.

In March of 1879, Tesla's father Milutin Tesla heard about Tesla living as a recluse and went to visit with him. He entreated with him to return to their home in Gospic and stay with them for a while as he saw that he was not doing so well.

Tesla seems to have politely declined. He was however brought to the hometown sometime later for some minor rule infraction in the local municipality.

After his return, Tesla began to feel better. His father, however, was ill and soon died of his chronic heart ailments. This was an event of great sorrow for Tesla. It seems to have rekindled a forgotten passion for proving himself to the world.

His uncles pooled their funds and sent him to Prague in 1880 to continue his studies and seek any employment that might come to him. He could not attend the university due to the requirements of needing to know Greek. It was not a total loss however as Tesla took to the library and also participated in some lectures in philosophy that he found very meaningful. The lectures in philosophy also seem to have deepened his appreciation of the creative process.

In 1881, he soon found work with an outfit in Budapest, Hungary at the telephone exchange. This is where his career of innovations is said to have officially begun. He served as a draftsman and then as the chief electrician. He excelled in this role and is said to have improved the phone amplification system. These ideas, however, were never submitted for a patent.

In the next year of 1882, Tesla got a job with an American Company out of Paris France. It was called the Continental Edison Company. His work comprised of installing the incandescent lighting bulbs across the city and for troubleshooting problems. He became quite skilled at solving problems in unique ways and the management took notice of this. They began to send Tesla to different facilities across France and Germany. Tesla gained much useful work experience during these assignments.

In the year 1884, a senior manager at the Edison Company, Mr. Batchelor was ordered back to the U.S. to help with the operations there. Mr. Batchelor recognized that Tesla might of great use there and insisted that Tesla accompany him and also meet the famous Thomas Edison.

And so began a series of events that brought two of the most prolific geniuses together.

Meeting with Edison and The Battle of the Currents

When Tesla came to the United States, he worked for about six months with the company and then met with the famous inventor Thomas Alva Edison.

At the prompting of Mr. Batchelor perhaps, Nikola went to Edison at his lab. Edison did not know what to make of the lanky young Serbian when Tesla handed him a note from Mr. Batchelor. This note simply read "I know of two great men, one is you and the other is this man".

Edison was impressed but did still not know what to make of this.

In those days, Edison's lab was the hub of frenetic activity. His electric company called Edison Electric had just begun to provide electricity to the homes of wealthy New Yorkers. This included notables such as Pierpont Morgan, a top financier, and banker.

There were problems with the wiring operations however and things were not going smoothly. There was a spate of short circuits and electrical shocks to animals and people. The streets had been festooned with a web of wires that hung like a Damocles sword over all who passed nearby.

During his meeting Tesla, Edison was distracted by runners from different parts of the city bringing messages about such problems.

So Edison did not know quite what to make of Tesla and of how he could help. He was about to dismiss him but then remembered a pesky problem he had been having with the lighting plant of a ship at harbor named the Oregonian. He asked Tesla if he could look into this and do something about it.

Tesla had heard much about Edison and wanted to make a good impression. He took his leave, rolled up his sleeves and went to work on the problem. He skipped sleep and was on the ship most of the night trying to figure out a solution to a problem that had evaded the engineers of Edison electric. He finally found the solution to the challenge and fixed the problem overnight. As Tesla emerged from the shipyard in the early morning with his tall Bowler hat, he was greeted by Mr. Edison who was also out for an early stroll with some of his staff. Edison remarked with some amusement of whether the "Parisian" had been out late taking in the nightlife. When Tesla explained that he had been working on the Oregonian most of the night and that the problem with the ship's powerplant had been fixed, Edison was truly amazed and thanked him. He told the companion after Tesla left that Tesla was a "damn good man."

A mutual respect and friendship was born and grew for some time. This, however, would not last.

There was increasing friction due to differences over their ideas for transmitting electricity, and about the viability of an AC motor that Tesla favored. Edison was already invested with the direct current model and asked Tesla to work on improving the DC motors in his company.

Edison and his company are said to have formally commissioned Tesla to perform for the sum of $50000 the job of improving the DC motor and its dynamos. Tesla agreed to work on the problem as desired by Edison.

Edison personally may have felt that such as feat of improving the DC motor was not possible.

Nikola went to work on the problem using both his logical, and intuitive manner. He worked tirelessly, sometimes through the night. After many weeks of hard work and ingenuity, he did the seemingly impossible and announced to Edison that the task of improving the DC motor had been done. Edison did not believe it at first but found it to be true.

When Tesla asked for the $50,000 that he had been promised, Edison acted amused and said that he was only joking and that perhaps Tesla did not understand American humor. He offered instead to raise his salary by $10 a week.

Tesla did not take this well. He had trusted Edison to be an honorable man that would keep his end of the bargain. He had been counting on the money to start his own laboratory. In bitter disappointment due to having been denied his promised payment, he resigned his position with Edison and left the company forever.

He went through a hard patch during the following year. In a twist of irony, the only job he could find was to dig ditches to bury Edison cable for 2 dollars a day. There is also some poetic metaphor here. Later events would prove that he would indeed "bury" Edison electric when the AC system of transmitting power overtook the DC system.

While Tesla was digging ditches that year, however, the prospects for his career in the United States seemed bleak. His fame soon singled him out to investors, and someone remarked to investors that a man of amazing intellect was wasting his time in manual labor in the suburbs of New York digging ditches. The investors were convinced of his potential and approached Tesla about providing him funds to support his research and to assist with the formation of a company of his own. Tesla took the offer.

Different Yet Similar

Tesla and Edison were polar opposites in a few ways but also remarkably similar in other ways. They were both identical in being geniuses of great talent. They both had a unique style of going about their work. Edison's approach was more helter-skelter, hands on at the get go and for throwing the kitchen sink at a problem. Tesla on the other hand was more nuanced and first tried to analyze the essence of the problem and planned a solution in his "mental laboratory" with details added and removed as his thoughts took him. He was able to visualize his project in his mind and could also test run his ideas in his mind. When he felt the idea would succeed, he would give it shape and test run it. Often times, his inventions would succeed the very first time. He said he was able to avoid much waste of effort by thinking in detail about his project before giving it shape.

Another difference was in their approach to violence and general ethics. While Tesla was invested in nonviolence and ethical behavior towards others, Edison was more pragmatic and pugnacious in his attitude towards the competition and anyone who came in his way.

There was also a difference in their attire and personal habits. While Tesla was immaculately attired and somewhat of a germaphobe, Edison was uncaring of his dress or personal hygiene.

Both men were similar in their superhuman drive and capacity for work. It was not unusual for them to skip a night's sleep if they were deep into their projects. While Tesla desired to go to sleep in a hotel room all his life, Edison would often go to sleep on an empty bench or table in his laboratory.

Tesla was well read with broad professional education in mathematics, electronics, and engineering. He also was well read in poetry, literature and the arts. Edison was self-taught and sometimes had a superficial level of knowledge, although he could focus in intently in the fields of his specific interest at the time.

Edison like Tesla was intensely curious and both could be stubborn.

In summary, both the men had differing and yet effective ways of working on problems. If both had been less stubborn about their views and had learned to work together, the world may have made even greater progress in the 20th century.

Tesla Tames Niagara Falls

In the 1890s, The Niagara Falls Power Project had begun, and Nikola Tesla was the main architect for designing the power generation and transmission system. People had thought for many decades about harnessing the power of the magnificent Niagara Falls. It was only with the help of Tesla that this dream came true.

The committee chosen for choosing the design team had been impressed with the demonstration of Tesla's ideas of the alternating electric current at the 1893 Chicago World's Fair. Tesla along with his investor George Westinghouse had made a splendid show at the event and demonstrated once and for all that the AC motor and transmission system was viable.

Once appointed, Tesla came up with intricate plans that still amaze the world. Many of his ideas were conceived and finalized in his head before putting them on paper. He conceived of the construction of an intricate set of tunnels that diverted the flow of Niagara River in order to turn turbines that would in turn power the giant AC dynamos. Huge turbines were created to his specifications, and gigantic motors were built separately. A system of stepping up voltage and stepping it down was created, and transmission wire was erected over many miles to Buffalo.

The physical energy given by the falls for turning turbines was converted with the help of magnets into alternating currents. These alternating electrical currents were more efficiently transmitted over long distances and lost less energy during transmission as compared to direct current. It was ideal for supplying power hundreds of miles away over cable wires.

The building of the Niagara Falls project was a landmark achievement not only for America but for the world. Transmission wires were erected for 22 miles to Buffalo, New York. Electricity had never been transmitted over such distances before. Intricate electromechanical equipment was built to the specifications of Tesla and thousands of skilled technicians, scientists and laborers worked nonstop for several years to complete the project. Many naysayers opined that Tesla's ideas were doomed and would never work.

George Westinghouse and to his credit had great faith in Tesla and both persevered despite the clouds of doubt that hung over the project like the dense Niagara fog.

When the switch was finally thrown at midnight on November 16, 1896, the system that Tesla had built worked like flawlessly. Like a charm, it carried power all the way to Buffalo New York and lit up the night.

Soon thereafter, power lines were constructed to New York City, and the Niagara Falls started lighting up the homes there.

The electrical systems that Tesla conceived and then built have been called sublime by engineers and near perfect in their design. They are still in use and working perfectly after all these years.

The taming of Niagara Falls, if nothing else, could serve alone as a crowning life time achievement for Nikola Tesla.

A System of Circling Satellites

Tesla conceived of a "Mechanical Eye" that "will be one of a group of associated machines that will teach a man to understand man." Tesla also conceived of modern-day satellites for purposes of communication. Many such satellites are now placed in geosynchronous orbits around the earth. Geosynchronous means it stays in position above the earth by keeping pace with the rotation of the earth. He also conceived of machines in the Earth's orbit that could transmit power to any point on earth by utilizing the charged upper atmosphere of the earth called the ionosphere. His vision for an information satellite or "mechanical eye" was realized decades later by the work of the great philanthropist scientist Arthur C Clarke.

Tesla and Radio Waves

Radio waves are electromagnetic vibrations that were first detected in 1873 by Clark Maxwell. German scientist Heinrich Hertz verified these in the year 1878. This was around the time that Tesla was working on his AC power systems. Tesla consulted with Heinrich Hertz, but the two could not entirely agree on how these waves were produced or transmitted.

He met with another scientist at the time named William Crookes and exchange ideas about how frequencies could be used to transmit information.

In 1893, Tesla demonstrated a system that we call radio today. The ideas used in this system were also used for wireless transmission by Marconi. Many believe therefore that Tesla should have shared in the awards and honors that were given to Marconi for the wireless communications that achieved with the help of ideas that Tesla had already filed a patent for. There was a contentious debate about this that went on for many years. Tesla was bitter about this and even called Marconi a "donkey" with no original ideas. The US patent office granted Tesla the patent for the radio as he had filed it earlier and rejected the patent filed by Marconi. In 1943, the United States Supreme Court name Tesla as the primary inventor of the radio.

Tesla and X-Rays

It is widely believed that Wilhelm Roentgen discovered x-rays in 1895. It was soon found that Tesla, in fact, had produced the x-rays in his laboratory sometime before this. He had taken x-ray pictures of metallic cylinders with their contents inside them, as well as radiographs of a hand and a foot. The subject of these X-rays is said to have been the author Mark Twain.

Tesla and Telegeodynamics

Tesla was intrigued by the phenomenon of resonance and amplification. His Tesla coil was built on this principle. He also experimented with mechanical vibrations that could amplify the physical effect at a distance. This field of study was called Tele geodynamics. Tesla's ideas were initially mocked and not well understood. It was only much later that the ideas were found to be viable and became a basis for prospecting for underground oil. He, however, was never fully acknowledged as the originator of the idea.

Remote Control and Tesla

In 1898, Tesla filed for a patent named "Method and Apparatus for Controlling Mechanism of Moving Vessel or Vehicles." It was granted that year, and he made a full demonstration of this at the Madison Square Garden by remotely controlling a small boat with a wireless remote control in his hand. Many were amazed at how he could turn the boat around and make it do various maneuvers by manipulating some levers in his hand. This technology was not utilized by the military initially but later came to be fully accepted as a means of waging war from a distance. Tesla also had other ideas for automating robots to carry out specific tasks through remote control. His thoughts and ideas were however ahead of his times, and he often found that his views were discarded. It was only much later that wireless radio control was adopted for many different applications in times of peace and war.

Tesla and The Internet

Tesla proposed to J Pierpont Morgan an idea for the wireless transmission of data to all parts of the globe through wireless technology. He thought the transmission of voice, pictures, private and military messages was possible through wireless communication. He also still believed in the wireless transfer of power all across the globe by energizing the ionosphere around the earth. J Pierpont Morgan appears to have been interested in the first idea of transmitting information while Tesla was more interested in the latter idea of transmission of electricity without wires.

The transfer of, electricity was after all his lifelong passion. Tesla, therefore, poured most of his energy while working in New York at Wardencloyffe Tower that he constructed for just this purpose.

When Morgan found out about the idea of transmitting electricity cheaply, he was not as excited as Tesla was. It has been opined that he and the other investors wanted to monetize electricity and not give it for free.

Whatever the reason was, the funding for the Wardencloyffe Tower project was withdrawn and everything fell apart on this project. If there had been better communication between the two men, and focus on one project at a time, perhaps greater success could have been realized.

The Bladeless Rotary Turbine and Tesla

Tesla came up with a very creative turbine that used the viscosity of fluids to transmit power. This turbine was a definite improvement over the existing models. For this very reason, there was considerable resistance in the industry to the adoption of his turbine. Both General Electric and Westinghouse had already invested large sums of money on their existing bladed turbine designs. They feared that these investments would be undermined if the new model proposed by Tesla became popular. It is said they therefore tried to discredit his innovation. His designs therefore never found much traction in the industry.

However, since the 1980s, the bladeless turbine has found widespread use in many different fields including mines and oilfields. During his lifetime, however, his intervention was relegated to the background, and he never received any financial profits from this brilliant invention.

Tesla And The Vertical Takeoff And Landing (VTOL) Aircraft

This was one of the last patents that Tesla received. It was a design for the vertical takeoff and landing of an aircraft in remote areas. The conceived aircraft would travel and land and take off vertically like a helicopter, tilt its rotor wings and then fly horizontally like a plane. Much later, on the basis of this design, the Osprey Aircraft shown above was created. It is now the workhorse of the U.S Marines. A similar plane is also use by some other countries. England also leveraged the concept when it built its Harrier Jets. This VTOL technology allows such planes to land without the need of a runway. The VTOL plane offers a tactical advantage for moving troops to remote areas where there are no runways. It also makes it possible for landing the plane on smaller battleships.

A Generous Spirit

As mentioned, it was Tesla's dream to make electricity freely available to everyone so that humanity could move forward together. He did not believe in unbridled capitalism that would serve to enrich only a few at the cost of others. It was Tesla's deep conviction that people would be able to create a more beautiful world through their creativity if their basic needs such as food, shelter, water, education, power, and healthcare were assured. He felt that this would also cut down on useless warfare and violence.

Tesla understood the magnificent balance in nature after having lived in the woods in his late teenage years to escape conscription into the army. He understood that we should not perturb it through the crude harnessing of energy that pollutes the atmosphere.

Driven by Ideas

Tesla was consumed and obsessed by the object of his interest. He was passionate about all things electrical. When he was attending the Polytechnic engineering college, he studied day and night to learn as much as he could. This obsession often meant that he would go nights without sleep and days without meals.

This high degree of absorption is a hallmark of his genius. It is a trait shared by other men of high talent. An Indian mathematician named Ramanujan also had the same passion for mathematics. Edison too was passionate. The force of ideas is remarkable when they take a hold of the imagination.

Tesla was in a state of creative bliss when he was working on a project. During such periods, it is said that he did not feel the hunger and fatigue until it would suddenly overwhelm him. In his own words, he was the happiest when he was working on his ideas and bringing them into reality.

There may be a lesson here. It could that if you want to be great at something, build an overwhelming obsession and passion towards it. It will provide you a wellspring of energy, strength, and joy that will shield you from distractions. Be so obsessed and passionate about your goals that all other concerns fall away. To avoid missing out on something, hire an assistant if you can to take care of the mundane things or details that don't need your level of skill.

A Love of Solitude

Tesla could be socially engaging when he wanted to be but preferred solitude over socializing. He was tall and generally well dressed and was sought out by women in social circles. Despite his own attraction towards them, he could not get any traction in any of his romantic relationships.

One of the obstacles may have been his aversion to touching hair. He also had habits that were of a ritualistic nature. For example, he would count the various steps of the dining process and then try to numerically coordinate the actions in multiples of threes and sixes.

Several women professed their love for Tesla but he was never able to break out of his shell and acknowledge the mutual feelings. A relatively famous French actress had expressed feelings for Tesla, and he had feelings for her in return. In his later years, he I had a wistful recollection of this and felt that it may have been a good idea to have had a life partner to ease the loneliness of his later years.

Tesla sublimated his need for companionship into his rigorous work schedule. On his downtime, he showered his kindness on pigeons that he fed every day. He also took helping to heal any injured birds.

The elite of society knew about his brilliance and associated quirks. They often invited him to social functions which he sometimes attended. During these events, he was able to carry himself with some aplomb as they were formal occasions and the structure of such events was more comfortable for him.

It is possible that Nikola could have been more sociable and used his famous will to overcome his social anxieties. If he were alive today, it is possible that certain medications that effect the serotonin system in the brain could have helped him.

The take away lesson is that he could have been more successful if had also conquered his social anxieties and shared more of his personal life and views with others. It is exceedingly hard to succeed in life by being a hermit no matter how brilliant one is.

The other view is that he was successful in his own way and the friends that he made were true. They loved him for who he was. His ideals and values were pristine and he is respected and honored for these today. Perhaps, it is better that he remained who he was and not some glib socialite trying to blend in and become one of the crowd. Perhaps we need more people like Tesla who are not afraid to stand out from the crowd.

Sensitivity to Stimuli

Nikola was unusually sensitive to sensations of sound, touch, texture, and light. He also experienced what we now know as synesthesia or a melding of the senses. He also experienced visual hallucinations and flashes of light at certain odd moments throughout his life. He did not like physical displays of affection although he could be tender with his relatives he was greeting after a long absence.

Tesla and the Higher Power

Although Tesla was not ostentatious about his faith, he did believe in a higher power. He attributed his survival from life-threatening situations to this God. He felt a higher power was personally vested in his survival and wellbeing. Tesla was influenced by renowned Indian spiritualist, Swami Vivekanand and felt that the Hindu ideology resonated with some of the higher truths of physics. Like another scientist, Michael Faraday, he believed that although God was not fully knowable, his works could be discerned.

Tesla and the Need for Financial Education

Tesla for all his wits was not financially sophisticated. He was quite trusting and was compassionate beyond reason at times. If Nikola Tesla had not abdicated his interest in the ongoing revenue stream from Westinghouse, he would have retired as a multimillionaire, if not a billionaire. As legend has it, when George Westinghouse shared his personal anxiety about the financial state of his company, Tesla told him he could help him. He then proceeded to tear up the financial agreement between him and Westinghouse. This treaty had obligated Westinghouse to provide him a royalty for every unit of electricity generated with the help of his inventions.

Thomas Edison, on the other hand, was quite astute and sophisticated about the financial value of his inventions. He marketed his ideas well and priced them to meet the market demand.

Tesla became increasingly impoverished in his later years and stayed in different hotel rooms. A compassionate patron, some say, Westinghouse helped with the hotel bills in his later years.

Take away lesson: One should be educated about the financial value of one's ideas and be willing to accept the reward for original ideas and creativity.

The Practice of Visualization

Nikola Tesla had a unique ability to visualize concepts and ideas. It is said that he could construct instruments in his mind's eyes and even run these virtual machines according to the laws of motion that he knew to see if there was any flaw in the design. Nikola Tesla attributed this unique ability to visualization games that he practiced. This involved the conceiving of various geometric shapes of different colors and morphing and changed them in his mind's eye. His father also had a unique game that he liked to play with him of trying to guess each other's thoughts.

The take away lesson from this aspect of his life is that the visual domain of our lives occupies a large part of our consciousness. It is useful when thinking of things to have a visual depiction of the concepts. We can use a simple paper and pencil to draw our ideas or use clay or other objects to depict our problems and problem scenarios in a physical form. This gives us a visual perch from which to conceive of the solutions to our problems. To the extent that we can visualize things and reduce them to their concrete form, these problems may become more pliable and more amenable to solutions.

Generating Ideas

"Be alone, that is the secret of invention; be alone, that is when ideas are born." ~ Nikola Tesla

Nikola Tesla was an advocate of finding silent spaces to nurture creativity. He felt solitude, quiet reflection and visualization can foster the emergence of inner knowledge and insight. He further believed that there was a universal storehouse of knowledge and wisdom that can be accessed by being adequately tuned for it. Nikola Tesla during his youth was sent into the backwoods by his parents so that he would not be conscripted into the army. They had already lost a son to the horse riding accident and did not want to lose another one to senseless warfare. During this period, Tesla found solace and comfort in the woods. He was in tune with nature and survived by hunting.

The lesson here is that it is essential to have a quiet place to study and reflect. This usually increases creativity and productivity.

To gain this silent space of creativity, a silencing of the mind should be obtained through activities such as meditation, showering, being in nature, walking, travelling or taking a drive on a scenic road.

A simple walk can be a great way to create some solitude. Einstein also seems to have had his best ideas when he was alone pushing his baby stroller or going for a stroll near his workplace. He would often carry a notebook and jot down ideas as they came to him. We now have cell phones into which we could dictate any ideas that come to us or create a voice memo for the same purpose of capturing ideas.

Doing something comfortable which does not require a lot of conscious effort may be the best way to tap into the unconscious wellsprings of latent knowledge and insight.

Value of Intuition

Tesla thought of intuition as an inborn ability that all human beings possessed to varying degrees. He also felt that it could be cultivated and developed. The below quote is attributed to him. His father would play games with involving intuition.

"Instinct is something which transcends knowledge. We have, undoubtedly, certain finer fibers that enable us to perceive truths when logical deduction, or any other willful effort of the brain, is futile." ~ Nikola Tesla

Nikola Tesla was indeed in tune with his intuitive abilities. A part of this ability appears to have been related to his ability to meld his senses. He was acutely sensitive to noise, smells and textures in his environment. This may have created a kaleidoscope of different inputs that generated a continuous wealth of ideas.

Following Your Passion

"When natural inclination develops into a passionate desire, one advances towards his goal in seven-league boots." ~ Nikola Tesla

In this quote, Nikola Tesla is using an expression seven-league boots from European folklore. These boots are often presented in a fairytale by a magical character to the hero of the tale. These boots allow the person to traverse great distances at high speed to complete an important task.

Nikola Tesla's passion was the harnessing of electricity and its transmission from one place to another. He devoted his entire life to this pursuit and achieved great success. He aligned his actions by studying physics and engineering at some of the most prominent universities in Europe. While there, he devoted himself to learning as much as he could about electrical phenomenon. If he had not been passionate about his interest, it is unlikely that he would have achieved all that he accomplished.

Takeaway lesson: Do some soul-searching and find out what your inclination is and what sets your soul on fire. Look at what comes to you naturally and when you are the happiest. This may be where in your talent lies. If you can align your actions and efforts with your natural ability, your chances of success will be greatly multiplied.

If you have an aptitude for numbers then develop an interest in mathematics or accounting. If you have a talent for science, then dive deep into it. If you have an ability for the written word, then jump into writing and learn as much as you can about that craft. If you are concerned about advocacy and social justice, then pursue a career in law. The choice of a career like a marriage is often a lifelong commitment. It should not be an arrangement of convenience but something borne out of true passion, love and conviction.

A passionate pursuit of your goal is almost always the royal road to success in almost every situation. Rare is the case when success comes by accident.

Science for the Common Good

"What we now want is closer contact and better understanding between individuals and communities all over the earth, and the elimination of egoism and pride which is always prone to plunge the world into primeval barbarism and strife... Peace can only come as a natural consequence of universal enlightenment..." - Nikola Tesla

Nikola Tesla was interested in Universal Peace. He advocated for mutual compassion and respect. He advocated for the provision of basic needs for all human beings including free power and electricity. When our basic needs are met, we are less likely to engage in harmful behaviors towards others. Nikola Tesla was an advocate of education and investigation into the forces of nature in order to harness them for the good of all mankind. He felt that once we were able to do understand and harness nature, there would be universal peace.

The unfettered greed of some is ultimately driven out of fear. Money is seen as a hedge against misfortune.

He saw money as a means to an end.

Some would say that his views were naïve and utopian. It is these views however borne out of high idealism that endears Tesla to a new generation of thinkers.

Tesla & Books

"Of all things, I liked books best." Nikola Tesla

Tesla was a fond reader and absorbed knowledge on all things related to the topic of his interest. He knew and spoke several languages. He would look up books in different languages to gain different perspectives. Books were a catalyst for thought and a source of new ideas for him.

He was not a passive reader and put the ideas he learned into action whenever he could.

There is a lesson here if one is willing to dwell on this fascination with books. It appears that the reading habit and love of books is directly tied to the level of achievement in our lives This appears to be borne out by facts as some of the most accomplished people in our era. It is a well-known fact that the current icons of achievement read on a regular basis. This includes the likes of Bill Gates, Warren Buffett and Elon Musk, amongst others. They regularly tap into books to broaden their understanding of their business and the world at large.

You too can benefit by befriending books and making them your trusted companions. Honor this relationship by creating a study area in your home if you can. Set aside a regular time for learning. Books can be read in the traditional paperback or nowadays on Kindle, Ibooks or other formats. A popular form for the busy commuter is audiobooks. Audible.com sells books in the audible format at reasonable rates. There may be other vendors of audible books as well. If you subscribe to YouTube Red, you can stream recorded audiobooks on YouTube for free. Blinklist is another company that provides summaries of great books in audio and written format for a very nominal fee.

Another clue to success is Tesla's habit of acting on the knowledge he acquires. You too should make a habit of acting on ideas that seem logical to you. The difference often between mere thinkers and very successful people is the habit of acting on their ideas and hunches at the appropriate time. This takes courage and some pluck, and this too can be cultivated and developed. Merely reading books and gaining ideas will not make much of a difference in your life or the world if these ideas are not acted upon. In summary, read, learn, discuss, plan and then act when you can. This is a lesson that is somewhat hidden in the life of Tesla.

Perseverance is a Virtue

"The scientific man does not aim at an immediate result. He does not expect that his advanced ideas will be readily taken up. His work is like that of the planter—for the future. His duty is to lay the foundation for those who are to come, and point the way." - Nikola Tesla

Nikola Tesla had several setbacks during his career. In his youth, he contracted a severe illness that lasted many months. Even though he experienced many hardships and faced resistance from his father, he continued to foster the dream of pursuing higher studies in physics and engineering. He persevered and finally gained a promise from his father to become a scientist instead of a pastor. Even in his moments of despair, he clung to hope. During his fallout with Edison, he was left penniless and had to dig ditches for two dollars a day to survive. He did not give up and was able to find collaborators with whom he formed his own electric company. During midlife, his laboratory containing many of his writings and papers along with his inventions burned down to the ground. He did not get bogged down in moping but soon organized a plan to recover the lost ideas and papers together. He soon was able to resume his work with a renewed vigor. He was able to recreate most of what he had lost. The effort had the effect of providing him a deeper understanding of his projects and yielded new ideas for new projects. This all occurred because he did not give up and persevered.

Takeaway lesson:

One must be persistent and exercise patience and resolve when there are setbacks. It is often the darkest before the morning dawn. Have faith that your efforts will bear fruit and continue to persevere towards your goals. Break any tasks that are remaining into subtasks and have an attitude of playfulness while you go about finishing the smaller subtasks. It is also wise to consult other people that may be able to offer you useful advice. Avoid negative people and naysayers who have grown comfortable in their failures. Seek advice from people that have achieved a level of success that you aspire to. Know when to fold on a dead-end project and look at your options again. It is ok to cut our losses and begin again. As long as there is breath, there is hope. Be hopeful and start anew. Always believe that you can achieve your goals.

Asperger's Syndrome and Tesla

Some say that Nikola Tesla may have had a variant of autism called Asperger's syndrome. This condition is marked by some character traits that were evident in Nikola Tesla. For example, he was acutely sensitive to sensations related to light, sound, touch, and smell. He could not stand the touch of human hair and was also uncomfortable with displays of affection such as hugging or kissing. His manner of relating to others was formal and at times stilted. He described his fascination with certain types of sharp geometric shapes and edges in jewelry and liked the glittering gems. He also felt a need to do things in a certain sequence and manner. For example, he liked to do things in sets of threes or sixes in order to feel comfortable. He had a fixed schedule for eating and expected the waiter to serve his dinners in a certain order and manner. He also tended to circle his hotel building a certain number of times before going in. Such obsessive-compulsive personality traits can be a feature of autism spectrum illnesses. Despite such limitations, the individual can possess phenomenal memory or other cognitive abilities that are extraordinary. Tesla did indeed have a photographic memory and a stellar intellect that was able to probe the depths of the electromagnetic phenomenon.

Take Away Lesson:

We must learn to honor all human beings even if they may be different from us or appear act in a manner that is different. They may have unique talents that can be helpful to others. Even if they don't have unique talents, everyone is worthy and deserving of respect as human beings.

Productive till the End

Nikola Tesla was actively engaged in continuous study and reflection even in his last days. He remained productive till the very end. He was working on number of advanced ideas at the time of his death. Many felt that his best days had passed him during his last years but they were proven wrong. Scientists are now finding that the ideas he was working on in his final days were visionary and decades ahead of his time.

Some of the projects in his last days were as follows:

A way to propagate electricity by wireless means.

A way to amplify the force of physical waves. This work was later instrumental in devising "ground thumping techniques to map the layers of earth in geological investigations.

A way to use lasers to focus energy at long ranges

A system to encrypt information during transmission over long distances. This later evolved into a data encryption process called "method of individuation".

There may have been other unknown projects. After his death, his papers were confiscated and held at the highest security levels. It is possible that some of his ideas are still open to investigation but still classified.

A Hero in His Homeland

Nikola Tesla died on January 7, 1943 in room 3327 of the hotel New Yorker. The room is now commemorated with a plaque and is visited at times by curious tourists. This was his final abode in the last years of his life. The autopsy revealed that he died of a blood clot in one of the coronary arteries that supplied his heart.

The U.S. government secured many of his unpublished papers and notes as they were thought to be of the highest value. Moreover, there was an apprehension that a foreign government might take advantage of his ideas and use them against the United States.

Many years later, the Ambassador from Yugoslavia requested that Tesla's mortal remains be returned for burial in his homeland. This request was granted and Tesla's body, some of his writings and personal effects were returned to Yugoslavia. Some Tesla biographers believe that the most sensitive documents were retained and not returned with the body.

He received a warm posthumous welcome in his home country. A wonderful museum was set up in Belgrade where thousands of people now go to pay their respects and to view his personal memorabilia. His childhood home has been reconstructed and restored to the way it was when Nikola Tesla grew up there. Many visitors make the trip now to the small village where he was born.

He is given great honor in his homeland and his birthday of July 10 is now celebrated as the Nikola Tesla day. Many other organizations around the world also commemorate the birth of this great man on that day. Fellow Serbians and other people of the region hold him in very high regard. His photograph has been placed on of the currency bills.

He Dreamed of a Peaceful World

Nikola Tesla was by nature a pacifist but he also understood the harsher realities of the world. He advocated for making war obsolete and impossible by arming each country so that they could defend themselves.

He talked about creating a robust system of lasers that could destroy legions of aircraft in the air or ships at sea. His concepts were memorialized as the "Tesla's Death Ray" invention in the popular Superman comics of the day.

Tesla's ideas of defense from space were seminal for the Strategic Defense initiative that has also been dubbed the "Star Wars Program". Some of the details of this program remain classified but significant strides have been made.

Tesla had seen the ugly side of warfare and was saddened by the wanton destruction of human life. Many individuals that lost their lives in war were often in the prime of their life. He felt that their talents could have been used for the betterment of humanity instead. He was optimistic about the future however and predicted that humanity would rise to meet the challenges that will arise in the future.

Projects Inspired by Tesla

TESLA, The Electric Car

Elon Musk conceived an electric car company named TESLA. The goal was to create an electric car that was affordable and reliable. The company has made significant strides and is rated highly for its performance. It is comparable in price to other midsize sedans. By making the switch over to an electric car, the threat of global warming from the burning of fossil fuel is likely to diminish. This is no mean feat when it succeeds. The financial success of the company will also provide funding for the other great Elon Musk company called SpaceX. The goal of SpaceX is to put a man on Mars within the next decade.

Saving Humanity by Colonizing Mars

Maiden Flight of the Falcon Heavy

Above is a picture of the maiden flight of the Falcon Super Rocket called the Falcon Heavy. This is the first step in the start of an epic journey to Mars. The Falcon Heavy can carry a big payload into orbit. The idea is to ferry construction equipment into space and build a base in space from where the BFR or the Big Falcon Rocket would start at the right time. The multistage ship would carry a crew of 60 to 100 passengers to Mars and then safely land on the surface of the red planet. The plan for the first trip to

Mars is evolving and everyone has high hopes for the project even though it faces many challenges.The first step in this phase is to launch a cargo ship in about four years from now in 2022. Soon thereafter, the manned ship will be constructed to allow for the transportation of passengers.

One of the challenges will be the protection of the astronauts from space radiation during travel and upon landing on Mars. The other challenges are those that are associated with weightlessness. The lack of gravity can cause muscle weakness, thinning of bones and a constant stuffy feeling in the head. Psychological challenges will also arise and will be related to separation from family and loved ones, the stress of a dangerous mission, and being in close proximity to others a long period of time.

These risks can be minimized with a proper selection of the crew and the training that they are provided. Other adjustments may also be possible to the space craft to minimize the physical risks.

Once there, the construction of a base will require creating living habitats possibly under the surface of Mars. Agriculture will need to be developed in order to make the colonies self-sustaining. It is an exciting and wonderful time to be alive on earth. Many innovative ideas are in the works for making the colony self-sustaining once it is established. Long term terraforming will also be initiated once the initial logistics are secured. Having a viable colony on Mars will ensure that the human race will survive any catastrophe that may befall planet Earth.

Tesla's Cosmic Conjectures

Around 1900, Nikola Tesla had conjectured on some ideas that seemed fantastic and ludicrous to some at the time. He felt that a layer of the upper atmosphere must be charged and that this charged layer could be used to conduct energy around the globe. Tesla in fact had filed for a patent for wireless transmission through such a region. Most people laughed off his idea.

In 1926 however, the British physicist ED Appleton did indeed discover that there was a layer of the atmosphere called the ionosphere that was charged. When another physicist in the 1980s named Bernard Eastlund filed for a patent titled "Method And

Apparatus For Altering A Region In The Earth's Atmosphere, Ionosphere And/Or Magnetosphere" it came to light that Tesla had already filed for a similar patent. This patent had remained sealed under a government secrecy order.

In the 1990s, this project evolved into what is known now as the High-Altitude Auroral Research Project or HAARP. It is located in the Gakona Alaska and is comprised of a vast array of huge antennas that are directing microwaves into the upper atmosphere at specific frequencies. The details of these projects are not known but have been inspired by the conjectures of Nikola Tesla.

In the future, it is possible that we will indeed find a way to realize that the dream that Tesla had conceived of using the upper atmosphere of the earth.

Epilogue

It is hard to conceptualize and reduce a complex and magnificent life to a few pages in a book. A human being is too complex for that. The lives of great men and women reveal some glimmer of their being and can illuminate our paths. We do have some biographical data about Tesla and we have tried to put together a mosaic of his life. It may seem disjointed but this great man had plenty of glimmer and glitter and there are lessons to be learned from his life.

Nikola Tesla was his own man. He was not perfect in every way but then no one is. The idea of a perfect human being itself a false one as we cannot judge a person by any one set of standards.

There are some markers of greatness however that run true in the lives of most men and women of eminence. It is perhaps a certain honesty in their soul that cannot be corrupted

Nikola Tesla was indeed such a person. Although beset with peculiar habits and ways; no one could doubt that there was a magnificent clarity to his soul.

He is also worth studying because he gave so much to the world through his ideas and work ethic. He is notable because he aspired like his factitious hero Abalfi to attain the higher virtues of our human nature. He is worth studying because he did not give in to despair but sought to improve the lives and fortunes of all his fellow human beings till his last days.

His attitude of challenging conventions and dogma continues to inspire successive new generations.

The generations to come do need a figure like Tesla because they will have to grapple with new problems. They will have to come up with ways to battle the growing threats to the world. These include short sighted policies that put profit over prudence when it comes to burning fossil fuels, a system that has corrupted democracy through the granting of citizenship to corporations. They will have come to grips with a growing world population and increasing fanaticism and retreat to tribalism as different cultures are challenged by the rapid changes of the 21st century.

Some of these visionaries have arrived on the scene; others will hopefully emerge in the next few decades.

More men and women of exceptional achievement are needed to ensure a better future for all of us. Nikola believed in mankind. He predicted that we would rise to the challenge and attain to our higher virtues; just like he did.

The End

Some Memorable Quotes from Nikola Tesla

"The scientists of today think deeply instead of clearly. One must be sane to think clearly, but one can think deeply and be quite insane." Nikola Tesla

"I do not think there is any thrill that can go through the human heart like that felt by the inventor as he sees some creation of the brain unfolding to success... such emotions make a man forget food, sleep, friends, love, everything." Nikola Tesla

"The history of science shows that theories are perishable. With every new truth that is revealed we get a better understanding of Nature and our conceptions and views are modified." Nikola Tesla

"If we want to reduce poverty and misery, if we want to give to every deserving individual what is needed for a safe existence of an intelligent being, we want to provide more machinery, more power. Power is our mainstay, the primary source of our many-sided energies. " Nikola Tesla

"Let the future tell the truth and evaluate each one according to his work and accomplishments. The present is theirs; the future, for which I have really worked, is mine." Nikola Tesla

"Electrical science has disclosed to us the more intimate relation existing between widely different forces and phenomena and has thus led us to a more complete comprehension of Nature and its many manifestations to our senses." Nikola Tesla

"Archimedes was my ideal. I admired the works of artists, but to my mind, they were only shadows and semblances. The inventor, I thought, gives to the world creations which are palpable, which live and work." Nikola Tesla

Akal Sahai!